BE STILL AND KNOW THAT I AM GOD
PSALM 46:10

66

70

Follow your feelings

Projects

Patterns

46

Welcome!

Welcome to the first issue of *DO Magazine!* We are so glad you found us.

Peg Couch, Editorial Director, Craft

We hope that, inside these pages, you will be inspired to color, craft, doodle, and draw. You don't need to be an artist, you don't need a lot of time, and you don't need to spend a lot of money to be creative. You simply need the desire to relax and get excited about taking the first step—after all, creativity happens one step at a time. The more you DO, the more you will enjoy DOing! This issue is all about coloring and patterning, so grab some colored pencils, markers, gels pens, or whatever you like, and get ready to dive in. We hope you enjoy the articles, projects, and coloring pages we've pulled together for you in this issue. We are incredibly lucky to have many talented authors to call upon to bring these ideas to you. Visit us on Facebook to post photos of your work. We'd love to see what you create!

Peg Couch
Peg Couch
Editorial Director, Craft

I DO craft!
DO Magazine is all about doing! Draw and color on these pages, tear out the coloring sheets, make something—have fun! Say, I AM creative, I DO craft!

DESIGN ORIGINALS

www.D-originals.com

Design Originals: DO Magazine – Color, Tangle, Craft, Doodle
Distribution by:
Fox Chapel Publishing Co. Inc.
1970 Broad Street, East Petersburg, PA 17520
Phone: 717-560-4703
Fax: 717-560-4702

Our Mission: To promote coloring, drawing, pattern ornamentation, and tangling for enjoyment and health

PUBLISHER	Carole Giagnocavo
CONTRIBUTORS	Suzanne McNeill
	Marie Browning
	Kati Erney
	Ben Kwok
	Joanne Fink
	Valentina Harper
	Thaneeya McArdle
	Jess Volinski
EDITORIAL STAFF	Peg Couch
	Colleen Dorsey
	Katie Weeber
	Melissa Younger
	Kati Erney
LAYOUT AND DESIGN STAFF	Ashley Millhouse
	Jason Deller
	Llara Pazdan
PROJECT DESIGN	Peg Couch
	Llara Pazdan
	Kati Erney

This book is printed on paper produced from trees harvested from WELL-MANAGED Forests where measures are taken to protect wildlife, plants, and water quality.

Forever Young at *Heart*

Carole Giagnocavo, Publisher, Design Originals

When I was an elementary school teacher, one of my greatest joys was encouraging each student's natural creativity. With adults, however, the creative process sometimes seems difficult. When we're young, we're uninhibited by accepted conventions. As we grow up, we somehow accept the (false) notion that we are not creative or artistic. This is simply not the case. A childlike creativity still lives in all of us, and that's what this magazine is all about. Whether you have an artistic or craft background or are just getting started, I know you can use the inspiration and instructions here to tap into your inherent creativity and make something wonderful!

This first-ever issue of *DO Magazine* covers the adult coloring book trend and meditative drawing. Design Originals has published Zentangle books (a meditative drawing method) for years, and recently produced more than 40 coloring book products. It's so fun to bring you the latest ideas in these blossoming trends!

Experts including teachers, therapists, and doctors are turning their attention to the benefits of patterning and coloring. Working through these pages will bring you calm and relaxed satisfaction, and it's so easy! Coloring and patterning activities can be done anywhere, do not require expensive supplies, and no experience is necessary. With coloring and patterning, there is no right or wrong, and therefore no pressure, just pure enjoyment. I know these activities will help you reconnect with the uninhibited creativity of your childhood. Explore feature articles showcasing the latest techniques, tear out a color sheet to practice right on the page, and check out the creative projects that will get your artwork off the page.

I hope you find coloring, patterning, and crafting with the ideas here as inspiring, fun, and fulfilling as I have.

Carole Giagnocavo
Publisher, Design Originals

My 85-year-old mother quilts and enjoys other crafts, but never tried coloring. She took to it quickly, and it's something she can enjoy doing with her grandkids.

Ranging from ages 11 to 80, adults and kids alike from my family enjoyed coloring activities at a reunion this past month.

A coloring book event held at our local Barnes & Noble bookstore featuring Peg Couch (Editorial Director, Craft) as a speaker drew a crowd of more than 100 people!

Botanical Coat Rack

Create a custom rack featuring one of your larger coloring works.
All you need to do is paint an unfinished wood blank from the
craft store, decoupage your design, and add a glass knob and
hanger. Wood blanks come in so many shapes and sizes—select an
interesting shape that complements your design. You can also use
this piece as handbag or scarf holder.

Materials:

- Colored design (pattern on page 87)
- Unfinished wood blank
- Glass knob
- White acrylic paint
- Lavender acrylic paint
- Decoupage medium
- Paintbrush
- Glue (strong adhesive)
- Picture hanging hardware

Project pattern by Valentina Harper

Tip!

If you are using a larger, door-sized glass knob, use the following technique to attach the knob. Measure the diameter of the hole in the back of the knob and drill a hole that size on the wood where you wish to attach the knob. Insert a wooden dowel (which fits snugly) into the knob hole and trim the dowel down so that the knob will end up flush to the wood when you slide the dowel into the hole in the wood.

1. **Prepare your coloring sheet.** Find the coloring template and cut the design to size. Color using your choice of colors and medium (we used standard coloring markers).

2. **Paint.** Apply two coats of white paint to the top of the wood surface, allowing the paint to dry thoroughly between coats. Paint the edge of the wood blank in a coordinating color (we used lavender), again with two coats.

3. **Add the design.** Apply a thin coat of decoupage medium to the back of your colored design. Be sure to coat the entire design. Position the design on the wood and, working from the center outward, gently smooth the paper onto the wood, flattening any bubbles that may appear. Allow it to dry. Next, apply a thin coat of decoupage medium to the entire surface of the wood. Be sure to cover not only your design, but also the painted area. Allow the decoupage to dry before adding one more coat of decoupage all over.

4. **Add the knob.** Decide where you want to place the knob. Apply a dot of hot glue in the correct place and press the bottom of the glass knob onto the glue. Hold it in place to set, and allow it to dry thoroughly. Then, attach your picture-hanging hardware per the package instructions.

Zentangle®

The Art Method That Changes Lives

Zentangle® is a mindful drawing method that pulls from patterns that can be found all around us in our daily lives, giving the art a natural feel that just seems right. The Zentangle method, created by Rick Roberts and Maria Thomas, is easy to learn, relaxing, and has the power to transform. Thousands of individuals practice the Zentangle method with thousands of different, positive results, including increased self-confidence, a new ability to focus and solve problems, and a rejuvenated sense of inspiration and creativity. Individuals have used the Zentangle method for pain management, to cope with mental illness, for meditation, and simply to take a break from a hectic life and relax. Practicing the Zentangle method is an experience that is unique to each person and their own life, and the positive results are tremendous.

Zentangle tile by Suzanne McNeill.

The Basics

You don't have to be an artist or have artistic talent to experience and create Zentangle art. Rick and Maria's trademark tagline "Anything is possible, one stroke at a time"™ sums up the entire philosophy behind the Zentangle method. While many of the patterns, or "tangles," of Zentangle may look complicated, once broken down, they are really only a series of lines, dots, and shapes repeated into a pattern.

The Zentangle method is meant to be relaxing. It frees your mind, instead of asking you to intently focus or concentrate on a complex task. Because of this, the basics of Zentangle are truly basic. Starting your first Zentangle piece is as easy as one, two, three: dots, connect, string. See page 7 for instructions on starting your first Zentangle piece. As you get

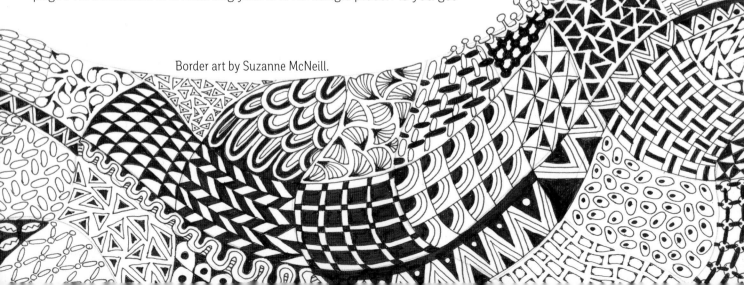

Border art by Suzanne McNeill.

started, keep the following things in mind:

There is no up or down. The beauty of a completed Zentangle piece is that it can be viewed from any angle; it has no top or bottom. Work on your Zentangle from any direction or rotate it as you work.

There is no right or wrong. Multiple people can draw the same tangles and the results will be somewhat different. There is no wrong way to draw a tangle. Have fun with them and make them your own.

There are no mistakes. Zentangle art is done in pen, without erasers or correctional fluid, because in Zentangle, there are no mistakes. If you place a line somewhere you don't want it in a Zentangle piece, just incorporate it into the design and keep going.

Zentangle Tools

To use the Zentangle method, you only need three tools: a pencil, a pen, and a piece of paper. While you can use any type of pencil, pen, or paper you desire, listed below are some products recommended specifically for Zentangle.

Pencil. Any No. 2 pencil will do. Find one without an eraser so you won't be tempted to "fix" your art.

Pigma® Micron 01 black pen. With pigmented, non-bleeding, archival ink, these pens are a dream for drawing.

Zentangle tiles. These 3½" (9cm) square tiles are made from fine Italian paper. Watercolor HP paper can also make a nice surface to tangle on, too. (Visit www.zentangle.com to purchase tiles.)

Zentangle extras. As you continue on your Zentangle journey, you may find some of these extras come in handy: a storage box to transport your supplies, a pencil sharpener, a Graphic 1 pen to make wider lines and for filling in areas with black, Pigma® Micron pens in colors, a white colored pencil or gel pen for tangling on dark paper, and blending stumps to help with shading.

When first learning the Zentangle method, keep it simple, and stick to the essential tools. The point is to focus your mind on the lines and patterns and not worry about what pen to use.

Step 1: Get Focused

The Zentangle method follows a few simple steps. Gather all your supplies together, and take a moment to just unwind. Try to clear your mind and breathe. Focus on the tools you have in front of you and the fact that you have this time to relax and achieve a feeling of peace. The blank tile is your space. It can become whatever you want it to be as you open your mind and achieve a sense of focus and concentration.

Step 2: Mark the Dots

Make a dot in each corner of your paper tile with a pencil. The dots create points with which to connect your border in the next step. You might also think of them as different aspects of your life, or a way to balance your tile.

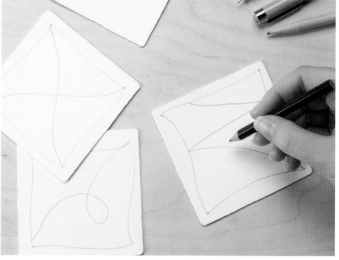

Step 3: Draw the Border

Using your pencil, connect the four dots from the previous step to form your border. You might think of your border as life's boundaries. Everyone's life needs some boundaries, and the border on a tile can represent these boundaries. That being said, everyone's life is different, so the border can be as individual as you are. You can make it with straight lines or curved lines—it's up to you.

Step 4: Draw the String

Draw a string with your pencil. The string's shape can be a zigzag, swirl, X, circle, or just about anything else that divides the space on your tile into sections. The string does not need to remain within the border you created during the previous step, but can extend off the edges of the tile if you wish. The string represents the golden thread that connects all the patterns and events that run through life. You can also think of each section the string creates as a different area of your life. The string will not be erased, but will disappear as you add your patterns. Avoid trying to force the string to have a desired outcome. Instead, let it flow onto your tile.

Step 5: Add Tangles and Finish Your Tile

Use a black pen to draw tangles into each section of your tile formed by the string. Rotate the tile as you fill each section with a tangle. When you cross a line, change the tangle. You may leave sections blank if you wish. Once you've filled as many sections of your tile as you desire with tangles, you can use your pencil to add shading and depth. Make sure you sign your finished piece—because it has no top or bottom, you can sign it anywhere. Then, sign and date the back of the tile. Take time to look at your completed art, and reflect on the peace and relaxation you felt while creating it.

Interested in learning more about the Zentangle method and the many amazing ways it can be used for fine art, crafts, and more? Check out *Joy of Zentangle* for an in-depth look at the story and practice of Zentangle plus a treasury of tangles; pick up *Beauty of Zentangle* to be wowed by a gallery of stunning pieces from Zentangle artists all over the world; or collect more than a dozen Zentangle series books to learn lots of tangles and craft ideas for Zentangle.

Learn Some Tangles!

Excited to start drawing? Here you'll learn how to create several popular tangles to get you started. As you can see, each tangle is built up in simple steps. After you've learned how to draw these tangles, you'll surely start seeing ideas for new tangles everywhere!

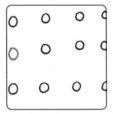  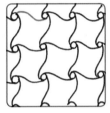 

Hollibaugh | Versatile—fill areas with black, patterns, or shading.
Tangle by Rick Roberts and Maria Thomas.

Cadent | Pops with shading!
Tangle by Rick Roberts and Maria Thomas.

 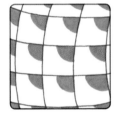  

Beelight | Better with a slight curve to the gridlines.
Tangle by Rick Roberts and Maria Thomas.

   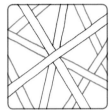

Weave | A very dimensional tangle.
Tangle by Karenann Young.

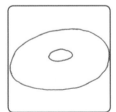  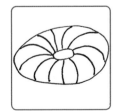

Tuffit | Try with the middle circle off center!
Tangle by Sandy Steen Bartholomew.

All things grow best when tended with h♥ve

Prayer Tangles

BY KATIE WEEBER

During years of sitting in hospital waiting rooms, Cindy Fahs found peace and healing through the Zentangle method

The Zentangle method of meditative drawing has grown and grown over recent years as more and more people discover its potential. Some people use it for creative expression, unlocking their inner artist. Some people use it for mental focus, to clear and sharpen the mind. And many people find it to be a healing, stress-relieving process. That's the case for Cindy Fahs of York, PA. Cindy spent thousands of stressful hours over a span of 13 years in hospital waiting rooms, dealing with her husband's worsening heart condition and waiting for him to get a new heart. Zentangle helped get her through those trials.

Cindy's favorite Zentangle book is *Joy of Zentangle*, and two of her favorite tangles are Flukes and all variations of Bales. There is a tangle out there to tickle anyone's fancy!

Flukes

Bales

"And I will give you a new heart with new and right desires, and I will put a new spirit in you."

- Ezekiel 36:36

Cindy combines the Zentangle method with her prayer time to quiet her mind and focus on one thing at a time. She says, "Before Zentangle, whenever I attempted to have true prayer and meditation time, God received my grocery list. Or the list of things I didn't get done that day, and the list of things I wanted to get done the next day. Nothing that entered my head had to do with quieting my mind and soul—the busyness of life got in the way."

Cindy started to feel frustrated and guilty when she couldn't turn her attention away from all of life's "to-dos," and eventually just stopped trying to have those quiet moments of prayer. When she combined the Zentangle method with her prayer time, however, she found the results were completely different. From the first moment she puts pen to paper, she can feel herself relaxing. By the time she's ready to fill her string with tangles, her mind and soul are ready to spend the time quietly.

Cindy says, "While I enjoy getting lost in the patterns of the tangle, my favorite part of tangling is drawing the string. For me, drawing the string is like taking the most relaxing big sigh and just letting everything melt away."

Though Cindy emphasizes that Zentangle isn't just for religious people—it can be a meditative and healing experience for anyone—she personally likes to use her prayer time to focus on a single Bible verse or inspiring quote. When she finds a verse or quote that resonates with her, she writes it on a sticky note

Cindy created this piece after receiving the good news that her husband, Scott, had been accepted onto the heart transplant list.

> *"No matter how I feel when I start tangling, by the time I'm done, the stress, everything, is gone, and I feel at peace."*

and puts it in her special prayer journal. When she's ready for her prayer time, she selects one of the verses and repeats it to herself as she tangles.

This practice was particularly helpful for Cindy when her husband, Scott, was waiting for a heart transplant several years ago. Cindy used her journal to spend time in prayer at doctor's offices and the hospital while waiting for test results and during Scott's successful surgery. Reviewing her journal, she can tell what was on her mind.

She says, "When I look back at a prayer tangle, I can tell how I was feeling at the time. If the design is very grid-like, I know I was feeling that some part of my life was out of control, and I was trying to put everything back into the box. If the design is very dark, then I was feeling stressed or angry. But

no matter how I feel when I start tangling, by the time I'm done, the stress, everything, is gone, and I feel at peace."

One piece Cindy did shortly after Scott's transplant surgery shows three interconnected hearts, representing the recipient (Scott), the donor, and the medical team. Says Cindy, "All three of those hearts are now intertwined forever."

Drawing had an unintentional side effect for Cindy, too, helping her to kick her smoking habit by giving her something to engage both her hands and restless mind. So whether you also have a family member in need like Cindy, or a stressful job, or simply want to step away from the overwhelming buzz of life, the Zentangle method may be just as helpful and healing for you as it was for her.

Cindy Fahs, a Certified Zentangle Teacher (CZT), lives in York, PA, and works at Fox Chapel Publishing. She can be reached at *cmfahs@gmail.com*.

Tips for Getting Started

For anyone who would like to try using the Zentangle method for meditation or prayer, Cindy gives the following advice.

Don't be self-conscious. "It's much easier said than done, but this is something that only you and God will ever see (if you want it that way). You don't have to share if you don't want to. Think of it as singing in the car—no one can hear you!"

Don't give up. "When I first starting tangling, the tangling stressed me out. I couldn't go to bed until I was done. The lines had to be straight, the tangles perfect. But the more I did it, the more relaxing it became, and I started to notice that the imperfections actually added to the tangles."

Let it all go. Surrender all the things that hold you back. The harder you try, says Cindy, the less beautiful and clean your piece will look—the lovely, stress-free flow really glows through the art, and you'll feel it, too.

When Cindy first started using the Zentangle method, she didn't really understand the meditative aspect—she used a ruler to plot out her designs and pressed so hard while drawing that she developed not only a callus, but a blister under her callus. This is one such design.

Show Off Your Work!

Everyone loves coloring, but what do you do with all of those pretty colored papers once you are done? Show them off! On these pages you'll find a whole host of great ideas for using your finished colored art. Patterns on pages 17-29 and 83.

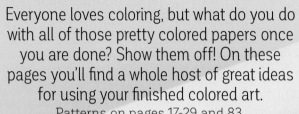

Project pattern by Jess Volinski.

Project pattern by Valentina Harper.

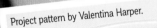

Project pattern by Jess Volinski.

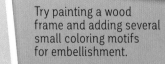

Try painting a wood frame and adding several small coloring motifs for embellishment.

Decoupage colored art onto glass and other surfaces!

Package baked goods in a pretty box and glue or tape a homemade tag on top. It's so simple, yet so special. You can even use store-bought treats—we won't tell!

Celebrate Your Love of Coloring

Make your next party the talk of the town by decorating with your own colored art! Here are some creative ways to embellish gifts, cards, and party accessories.

Make your own greeting cards by layering coloring designs onto pretty coordinating scrapbook paper. It's so much more personal and a lot less expensive!

Everything's better with a cupcake! Clip out a small colored design and tape it onto one end of a toothpick. Insert the toothpick into your cupcake and *voila*...you have a party!

Rethink the bow! Replace a store-bought bow with an adorable hand-colored gift tag. It's so much more personal and pretty!

Sometimes wrapping the gift is more fun than giving it! Here, solid color gift bags come to life with bright and chunky colored gift tags. Simply cut to size, layer on scrapbook paper, punch a hole, and attach with baker's twine or pretty ribbon.

What an adorable and inexpensive idea for your next party. Serve up pink lemonade in milk jars embellished with small colored designs. Add a paper name tag and fun straw. A party in a glass!

Project pattern by Valentina Harper.

Creative Framing Ideas for Coloring Enthusiasts

Here are some easy ways to use inexpensive frames and craft supplies to make beautiful wall art yourself. Use any pattern you want to create pieces like these. Who says you're not an artist!

Embellish a wood frame with your colored design. You can buy unfinished frames at the craft store and paint them in a coordinating color. Add a photo or favorite poem as shown here.

You can really make a statement by simply framing a favorite coloring piece in a big, chunky white frame. The color will really pop!

Project pattern by Valentina Harper.

Project pattern by Valentina Harper.

Project pattern by Valentina Harper.

These colored designs were clipped from the original page and then layered on top of scrapbook paper. What a great way to punch up the color.

Project pattern by Valentina Harper.

Project pattern by Jess Volinski.

Project pattern by Thaneeya McArdle.

Turn any standard notebook into a beautiful art journal or diary! Simply cut your colored design to size and use a decoupage medium to adhere it to your book. Add a favorite quote or message with a paint pen or marker.

Here is a fabulous craft idea to use with coloring. Cut one of your favorite designs to fit a standard bathroom tile. Use a decoupage medium to adhere the colored design to the tile. Finish with a coat of clear acrylic spray. Add felt feet to protect surfaces from scratching. Make a whole set!

Simple Handmade Gifts to Color

You don't have to be a fine artist or spend a lot of money to make handmade gifts. These super simple ideas made from coloring pages show that a little creativity goes a long way to make someone feel special.

Project pattern by Thaneeya McArdle.

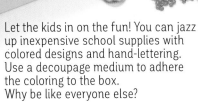

Let the kids in on the fun! You can jazz up inexpensive school supplies with colored designs and hand-lettering. Use a decoupage medium to adhere the coloring to the box. Why be like everyone else?

Add colored designs to ordinary candle holders to create something truly unique. They will look like they came from a fancy boutique! Such a beautiful gift.

Project pattern by Thaneeya McArdle.

If you run out of pattern pages in this magazine, or do not want to use decoupage on your artwork while crafting, all of these designs (and more!) can be found in our new, incredibly cute and fun series of color-your-own sticker books. Premade stickers are a perfect way to create a beautiful work of art, or to add a special little something to any project, with absolutely no hassle. You can find this series online at www.d-originals.com.

DON'T MISS A SINGLE ISSUE!
Subscribe Today and Save 30%!

color
tangle
craft
doodle

Subscribe & Today SAVE 30%

YES! ☑

SEND ME
ONE YEAR
FOR ONLY
$27.99

Send Me One Year at the Charter Member Subscription Rate

Annual Cover Price	Your Price
~~$39.95~~	**$27.99**

Canadian subscribers add $5.00, all other countries, add $10.00 (U.S. funds only). *DO Magazine* is published 4 times per year. Please allow 4-6 weeks for delivery of first issue.

Name: _____

Address: _____

City: _____

State/Prov.: _____

Country: _____ Zip: _____

E-mail: _____

☐ Payment enclosed   ☐ Bill me later

☐ Start my subscription with Premiere Issue #1

Subscribe & Today SAVE 30%

YES! ☑

SEND ME
ONE YEAR
FOR ONLY
$27.99

Send Me One Year at the Charter Member Subscription Rate

Annual Cover Price	Your Price
~~$39.95~~	**$27.99**

Canadian subscribers add $5.00, all other countries, add $10.00 (U.S. funds only). *DO Magazine* is published 4 times per year. Please allow 4-6 weeks for delivery of first issue.

Name: _____

Address: _____

City: _____

State/Prov.: _____

Country: _____ Zip: _____

E-mail: _____

☐ Payment enclosed   ☐ Bill me later

☐ Start my subscription with Premiere Issue #1

DON'T MISS A SINGLE ISSUE!
Subscribe Today and Save 30%!

color
tangle
craft
doodle

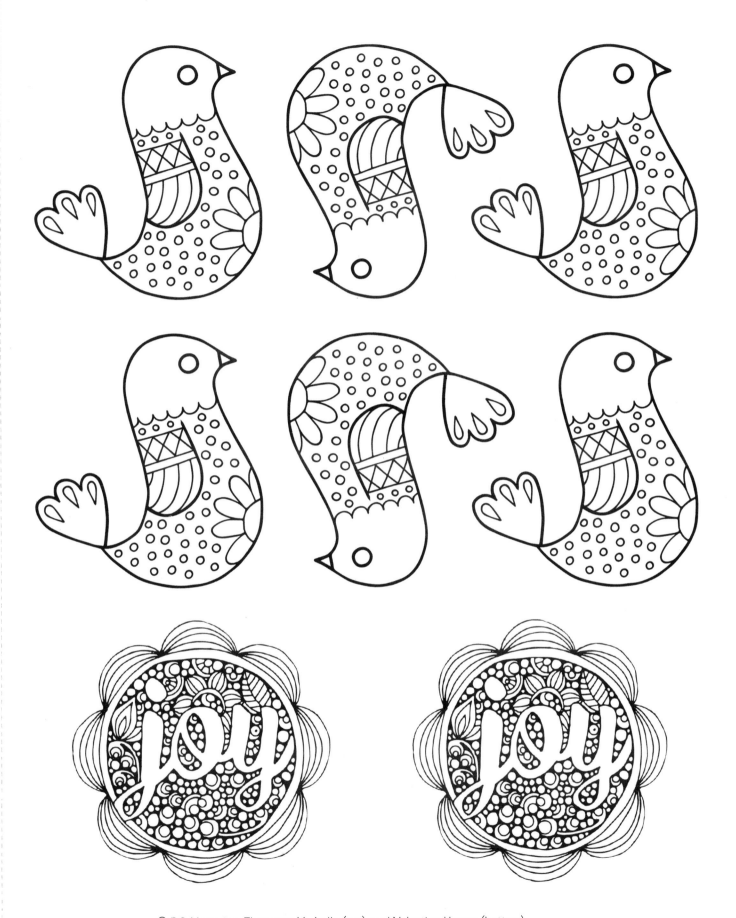

© DO Magazine, Thaneeya McArdle (top), and Valentina Harper (bottom)

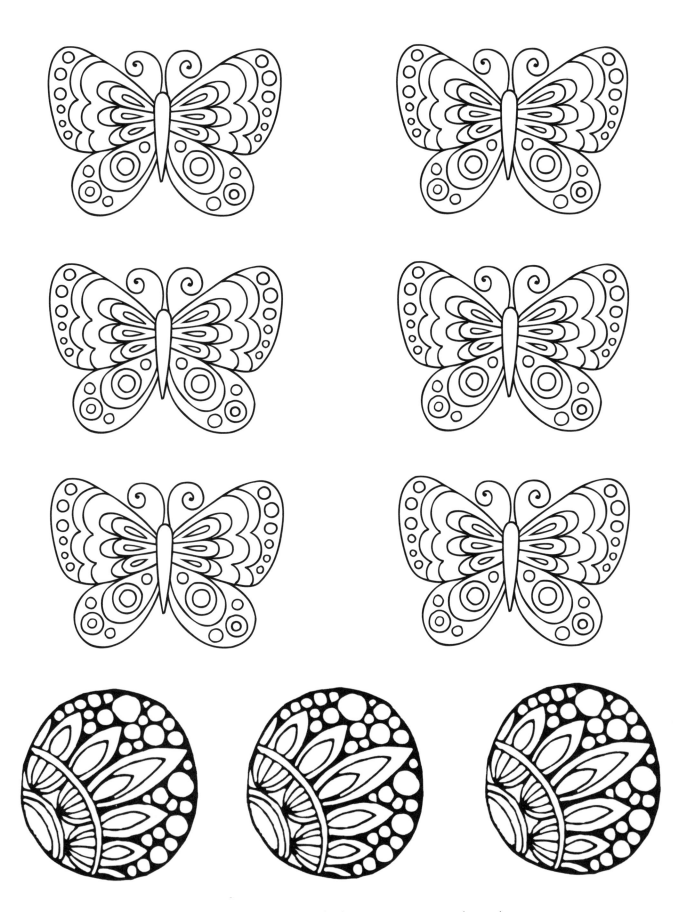

© DO Magazine, Jess Volinski (top), and Valentina Harper (bottom)

© DO Magazine and Jess Volinski

© DO Magazine and Jess Volinski

© DO Magazine and Jess Volinski

© DO Magazine and Valentina Harper

Cover Project!

Diverse Dragonflies

BY KATI ERNEY

What is one thing that can add pop and pizazz to any work of art in minutes? Color! All through school we learn what colors are, how to use them, and how to mix them; in this color study, I used the same dragonfly image, courtesy of the phenomenal artist Ben Kwok, to showcase ten different color schemes and patterning techniques with a variety of different art mediums. I was greatly inspired by the dragonfly colored by Marie Browning that's featured on the cover of this magazine; it made me want to try some colors of my own. The possibilities are endless, so turn on your imagination, grab a color wheel, and get going!

See pattern on page 49.

Analogous shades of blue and blue-green brush markers make a very pretty and aquatic dragonfly. Adding touches of black enhances the small details you incorporate into your design.

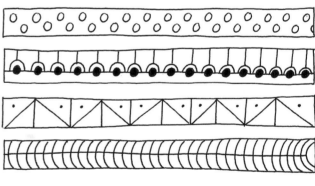

Not only can you color the designs in this book, but you can also add additional patterning to many of them! As you look at the dragonflies on these pages, you will see different patterns. Try some of the above patterns out on your own dragonfly!

Kati Erney works on staff at Design Originals in the book editorial department, where she spends a surprising number of hours crafting. She loves to color and pattern.

The tools I used to make these dragonflies included Sakura Koi brush markers, Crayola SuperTips washable markers, Artist's Loft colored pencils, and Fiskars gel pens. Experiment with your favorite brands!

I used brush markers and a complementary color scheme of magenta, neon pink, yellow, and light green to portray a bright and vibrant dragonfly.

I used a mix of pink and red colored pencils to create this dragonfly. The monochromatic use of color illustrates a romantic theme.

For this dragonfly I used black, fuchsia, and deep purple brush markers to test out a darker-themed piece. Darker colors do not stand out as well as brighter hues, but make for interesting combinations, as you can see in this moody piece.

Using only two brush markers in complementary colors, orange and blue, I created a highly contrasting dragonfly that is sure to draw the eye. The white space also helps to amplify the color.

Happy Halloween! This dragonfly is very thematic; its predominantly black and orange color scheme was achieved with both colored pencils and washable markers.

For this dragonfly, I used a strictly warm color scheme (red, orange, and yellow) that is representative of a brilliant ball of fire. Brush markers are perfect for seamless color.

Tip: When using a variety of different tools, especially an assortment of markers, try testing your colors before you let loose on your artwork. For example, Sakura Koi brush markers are very wet and rich in color, so using all dark hues on a detailed piece may leave your work muddled and hard to identify.

For this dragonfly, I chose the brightest gel pens I could find and went to town! Complementary colors are my favorite, and shades of purple and yellow give a very pleasing look.

Fellow colorist Llara Pazdan used a mix of gel pens and brush markers with many different layering techniques to create this off-the-wall, psychedelic dragonfly.

I used a combination of blue and green brush markers to achieve an earthy, nature-infused tone. Try using colored pencils on top of your markers to add dimension for an even more naturalistic look.

FloraBunda

FloraBunda is a new collection of simple, easy-to-draw, nature-inspired art doodles that you can use to create your own unique art.

Whether you already love drawing or have never thought of yourself as someone who can draw, you'll find the simple shapes of the flowers, leaves, and vines of FloraBunda easy to learn.

Relax your mind and let your creativity flow as you sketch, mixing and matching elements to create unique compositions. Then use markers, colored pencils, watercolors, or any favorite medium to magically transform your inky doodles into exotic, lively plants. Be eclectic, be whimsical. Enjoy yourself. In no time you'll be creating gorgeous art, and every piece you draw will be uniquely yours.

Draw-It-Yourself Designs

Each design is broken down into several straightforward steps that you can follow to build the completed design quickly and easily. Practice the steps in the squares provided, and learn to see the component parts in each design.

Make Your Garden Grow!

Create an overflowing garden by layering your FloraBunda designs! Go ahead—finish each of the vines on page 40 by following the example or planting your own flower ideas! Then color the full-page art on page 91.

Project: Painted Box

This chalkboard-esque box flips traditional drawing designs on their head by making them pop by using white on a dark background. Even an inexpensive wooden box looks like a million bucks once you give it this special treatment.

PROJECT BY KATI ERNEY

Materials

- Box (wood, plastic, etc.)
- Black acrylic paint or spray paint
- White acrylic paint
- Flat and liner paintbrushes
- Protective enamel spray

1 **Paint the box.** Paint the entire box black using either spray paint or acrylic paint and a flat paintbrush. Allow the paint to dry.

2 **Sketch the design.** Sketch your design on the box with a graphite pencil (if it shows up on the black) or a white colored pencil.

3 **Paint the design.** Trace the design with white paint using a liner brush. If you want to create a raised, puffy effect, go over the lines several times. Allow the paint to dry.

4 **Finish the box.** If desired, protect the finished box with a protective enamel spray suited for painted surfaces.

Suzanne McNeill, CZT is a gifted craft designer and artist. As the founder of Design Originals, she has written or co-authored hundreds of titles. Suzanne was an early fan of the Zentangle method and helped promote it by writing more than a dozen titles—including *Zentangle Basics* and *Joy of Zentangle*. She is the inventor/artist behind FloraBunda and has written *FloraBunda Style*, *FloraBunda Basics*, and *FloraBunda Woodland*. These are available to order (see page 77) and in craft and bookstores everywhere.

Catching Up with Suzanne McNeill

Suzanne McNeill has written hundreds of craft books on all sorts of topics, and was the forerunner in books on Zentangle, publishing many volumes in her Zentangle series before any other publisher had even gotten wind of the method. She'll be a regular columnist and contributor to *DO Magazine*, so look for more of her art in upcoming issues. We caught up with Suzanne to see what she'd been working on recently. Here are some snapshots of her latest pieces of art, as well as some tips and tricks for working with one of her fall favorites, gourds.

Tips for Working with Gourds

Whether you are going to paint or add tangles to a gourd, or be more ambitious and do any woodburning or carving, follow these important tips to find a good gourd and make your gourd clean and safe to work with.

- Good gourds have few blemishes and a smooth, not bumpy or scratched surface; look for them at farmers' markets.
- You can also purchase pre-cleaned, hollowed-out gourds online; just do a search for "gourd farms."
- You will want to use a face mask and eye protection, and possibly gloves, when cleaning, hollowing out, and/or sanding the surface of a gourd, as gourd dust—which typically includes mold—is not healthy to inhale.
- Prepare the surface of the gourd by soaking it in warm water for a few minutes and then scrubbing it with an abrasive tool like a metal scouring pad to get off all the gourd dust.
- If you want an extra-smooth surface, you can sand the surface of the gourd with fine sandpaper.
- Gourds are smooth and slippery even when dry—try drawing or painting on your gourd on top of a non-stick surface. You can cut a piece of non-stick shelf liner and simply place it on your work surface.

The patterns of giraffes' coats remind me of Zentangle. I overlapped several of these elegant animals in different sizes directly onto stretched white canvas with a big black PITT marker. Then I outlined the family of giraffes and painted the background with flat blue-green acrylic paint and with black acrylic paint. See more of the detail on this image on the back cover!

Sketching in museums and when traveling is always inspiring to me. Drawing preserves my memories and inspires me to look closely at everything. On a trip to Greece, we took a boat over to visit the ruins at Ephesus, Turkey. The ancient buildings, statues, carvings, and patterns were totally inspiring. While at the ruins, I sat down and drew this montage of my favorite images on Arches 140# HP watercolor paper with a black Sakura MICRON 08 pen.

Zentangle patterns are easy to draw on smooth gourds. I used a pencil to draw the outline of each pattern on each of these gourds. Next, I painted areas on each gourd with white acrylic paint (two to three coats) and let that dry overnight. I drew around the outlines and added tangles on the gourds with a black Sakura Graphic #1 pen. On the largest gourd, I painted part of the background with blue acrylic paint.

Color Burst Mandala Stool

Use your coloring designs to create one-of-a-kind home accents that will look like they are from expensive catalogs. This gypsy-inspired mandala stool was a flea-market makeover. The finished effect is fun, funky, and will spice up any room. Change up the colors to suit your own décor and preferences. The mandala design will also work well with platters, trays, and other circular items.

Materials

- Colored design (pattern on page 81)
- Stool (or other circular item)
- Purple spray paint
- Decoupage medium
- Paintbrush
- White paint pen

Project pattern by Thaneeya McArdle

1. **Prepare your coloring sheet.** Find the coloring template and cut the design to size. Color using your choice of colors and medium (we used standard coloring markers).

2. **Paint.** Apply two coats of purple spray paint to the stool, allowing the paint to dry thoroughly between coats. Be sure to paint all the surfaces of the stool, especially the spindles.

3. **Add the design.** Apply a thin coat of decoupage medium to the back of your colored design. Be sure to coat the entire design. Center the design on the stool and, working from the center outward, gently smooth the paper onto the wood, flattening any bubbles that may appear. Allow it to dry. Next, apply a thin coat of decoupage medium to the entire surface of the top of the stool. Be sure to cover not only your design, but also the painted area. Allow the decoupage to dry before adding one more coat of decoupage all over.

4. **Embellish with a paint pen.** Add some additional interest to your stool by embellishing it with a white paint pen. We have added a thin rule around the stool as well as polka dots on the legs. Be creative and add what looks good to you!

Patterning by
Sue Daves

Design Templates from the

Wild Side

Patterning and color by
Abbey Gray

Ben Kwok's templates for tanglers and colorists have spread like wildfire online

BY KATI ERNEY

Ben Kwok is a private, 35-year-old visual artist and designer from Los Angeles, California. His love for art, combined with his generosity for other artists, has made him a superstar on the Internet in the eyes of thousands of fans from all around the world. Ben has drawn more than 100 design templates that allow artists to tangle and color images ranging in subject from owls and wolves to antique ocean diving helmets and mandalas. The dragonfly on the cover of this magazine, as well as those featured in the article "Diverse Dragonflies," is an example of one of Ben's designs, more of which you can find on pages 49-55.

What Ben finds most interesting about the way artists and doodlers approach coloring and Zentangle art is that many of them prefer to start with a predetermined shape. He explains his eureka moment

as one where he realized that what he personally enjoys the most is creating the templates. There seems to be something special about them—designed by an artist for other artists. "While a lot of Zentangle art is abstract," he says, "there are also many [artists] who like to make Zentangle art in the shape of a particular object or animal. Many times these tanglers like to start from pre-existing layouts so they can focus on adding their intricate designs. ... I saw this part as one where I could be helpful, so I decided to start creating templates for Zentangle enthusiasts and doodlers. When they create their intricately patterned artwork inside my distinctive shapes, it seems like a perfect fit."

The response to Ben's templates was above and beyond what he could have imagined. "When I started creating templates like

these, I had hopes of building a community centered on them, but the feedback and love I received was completely unexpected," says Ben. "I had no idea the templates would be so popular, or that they would have such a positive impact on the lives of others."

Ben is currently looking at ways his popular wildlife designs could be used to support animal conservation, a topic he feels very passionate about. He is particularly attached to elephants and focuses his attention on the Save the Elephants project through the Wildlife Conservation Network.

To learn more about Ben and his fantastic artistic endeavors, and to get your hands on some original design templates, visit Ornation Creation on Facebook and *www. TangleEasy.com*.

Color by
Ben Kwok

Patterning and color by LeeAnn Denzer

Patterning by Darla Tjelmeland

Patterning and color by Johanna Garwood

Ben Kwok is a talented, detailed-oriented artist and designer who has worked with major brands including Disney, Converse, and Lucky Brand. His book *TangleEasy Wildlife Designs* is the first in a new series. See page 77 for information on ordering.

Rustic Wall Art

Here is a wonderful project for your fall decorating. It will not only add a warm touch of rustic elegance to your home, but it is so easy to create. Simply color and decoupage a leaf design onto a readymade wood slice (available at most craft stores). Add a burlap hanger for a nice finishing touch. It's that easy!

Materials
- Colored design (pattern on page 85)
- Wood slice
- Burlap ribbon
- Flat-headed tack
- Decoupage medium
- Paintbrush

_____

Project pattern by Valentina Harper

1 **Prepare your coloring sheet.** Find the coloring template and cut the design to size. Color using your choice of colors and medium (we used art brush markers).

2 **Add the design.** Apply a thin coat of decoupage medium to the back of your colored design. Be sure to coat the entire design. Center the design on the wood slice and, working from the center outward, gently smooth the paper onto the wood, flattening any bubbles that may appear. Allow it to dry. Next, apply a thin coat of decoupage medium to the entire surface of the slice. Be sure to cover not only your design, but also the entire front surface. Allow the decoupage to dry before adding one more coat of decoupage all over.

3 **Attach the burlap ribbon.** Cut a length of approximately 4" (10cm) of burlap ribbon and make it into a small loop. Attach the loop to your wood slice with a small flat-headed tack.

4 **Hang your art.** Use a small nail to hang your rustic art by the burlap loop.

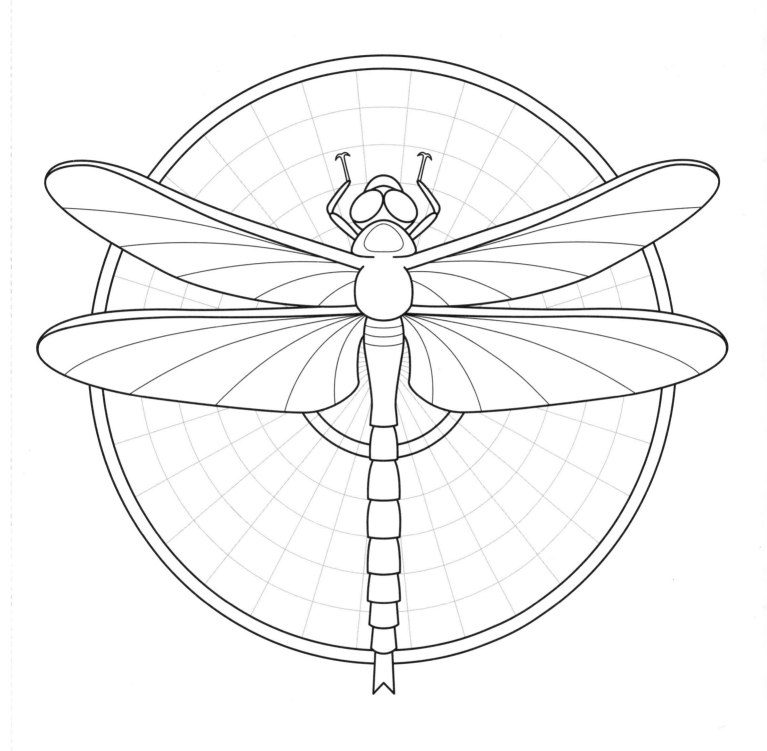

© DO Magazine and Ben Kwok

© DO Magazine and Ben Kwok

© DO Magazine and Ben Kwok

Mandala

Ohm

Yin-yang

Metatron's cube

Cross

Tree of life

ine and Ben Kwok

COLOR & CREATIVITY BY _____

Be Still
AND KNOW
THAT I AM
GOD
PSALM 46:10

©JOANNE FINK·WWW.ZENSPIRATIONS®.COM   COLOR & CREATIVITY BY _____

© DO Magazine and Joanne Fink

LOVE

A FRIEND LOVES AT ALL TIMES. PROVERBS 17:17

SING UNTO GOD ALL THE EARTH A NEW SONG PSALM 96:1

© DO Magazine and Joanne Fink

A World of ZENSPIRATIONS®

Joanne Fink loves to draw and letter to inspire herself and others. You may have noticed her work for its brilliant use of color, her distinctive patterning, and her trademark "dangles" designs.

Inspiring words and positive thoughts are always present in her art. Her passion for drawing is evident in the huge archive of work—thousands of images—she has created over the years. No matter where Joanne goes, she always has pen and paper with her as her ideas seem to flow endlessly. Zenspirations® create, color, pattern, play coloring books have evolved out of her archive and contain a beautiful mix of her work. Surprisingly, Joanne doesn't enjoy coloring in her books as much as she does drawing them, but that's okay—she has thousands of fans around the world who eagerly wait for the unveiling of each new book and are happy to add color for her!

Her latest coloring books, *Zenspirations Birds & Butterflies* and *Zenspirations Expressions of Faith*, are each filled with 32 pages of designs to color, as well as an inspiring gallery of colored images from her "coloring enthusiasts". You can get a sneak peek of some of the designs in this magazine! In Joanne's books, you discover new ways to express your creativity by adding color, patterns, text, and illustrations to extraordinary images. Printed on high quality extra-thick paper and with pages perforated for easy removal, each book is perfect for decorating with colored pencils, markers, or gel pens.

While you're waiting for these two new books to hit shelves, have fun coloring the special excerpts on pages 57-63, and check out Joanne's Facebook page dedicated to the Zenspirations world: *www.facebook.com/ groups/1471158256528576.*

Check out the currently available titles in Joanne's Zenspirations coloring book series! Pick up *Flowers* for a beautiful garden of floral and plant designs; try out the modern, stylish images in *Abstract & Geometric Designs*; and let the quote-driven *Inspirations* fill you with joy. Once you try one, you'll want to own them all!

In Joanne's coloring books, you get to see several different colored and patterned examples of a single design. These "color studies" are a fun and interesting way to get started with your own art! Above is just one example of a color study; you'll find more studies in upcoming issues of *DO Magazine,* such as ones for the two pieces of art shown below.

Joanne is always busy working on a new piece of art in her home studio in Florida.

Color study image credits: Top left tree illustration by Jennifer Priest; top middle tree illustration by Tracey Lyon; top right tree illustration by Gail Beck; bottom left tree illustration by Terri Brown; bottom right tree illustration by Ardis Ferdig. Dove illustration by Carisa Zglobicki. Owl illustration by Gail Beck.

Custom Switchplate

Turn on the color with a custom switchplate! This project is so easy, but really packs a lot of style. Designed to fit any standard switchplate, this craft will work for whichever room of the house needs a little extra pep.

Materials
- Colored design (pattern on page 89)
- Switchplate
- Decoupage medium
- Paintbrush
- Utility knife

Project pattern by Valentina Harper

1. **Prepare your coloring sheet.** Find the coloring template and cut the design to size. Note: at this point, only trim around the exterior border of the switchplate—do not cut out the holes for the switch and screws. Color using your choice of colors and medium (we used standard coloring markers).

2. **Add the design.** Apply a thin coat of decoupage medium to the back of your colored design. Be sure to coat the entire design. Center the design on the switchplate and, working from the center outward, gently smooth the paper down by pressing outward to the edges and over the bevel, flattening any bubbles that may appear. Allow the switchplate to dry. Next, apply a thin coat of decoupage medium to the entire surface of the top of the switchplate. Allow the decoupage to dry before adding one more coat of decoupage all over.

3. **Cut the holes.** Turn your switchplate over (top down). Use a utility knife to carefully cut the paper covering the switch and screw holes so that you have clear openings for the switch and screws.

4. **Attach the switchplate.** Center your switchplate on the designated wall area and attach the screws.

Bonus!

For an alternate look, create a decorative border around your switchplate using the pattern on page 89. (See the inset photo on the following page.)

Making Magic with *Brush Markers*

BY MARIE BROWNING

If you've never tried using water-based brush markers before, you are in for a real treat! These special markers' ink is perfect for blending, and most brush markers have a flexible brush tip on one end and a fine tip on the other end. The brush tip of a dual brush marker works like a paintbrush to create fine, medium, or bold strokes, whereas the fine tip gives thin, consistent lines. When you pair a marker with other tools such as a colorless blender or water brush, you can create an amazing array of beautiful effects! Here, you'll learn one popular technique plus how to draw freehand designs with brush markers.

665 NH — Color Designation Number

Brush Tip   Fine Tip

Here are just a few examples of the stunning effects you can achieve with water-based brush markers. Check out the book *Brush Marker Magic* by Marie Browning for all these techniques and more!

Tip: Some brush markers' brush tips aren't flexible, so check before using them for the drawing techniques on page 72-73. And make sure you have water-based markers, not alcohol-based, or blending won't work.

Direct to Paper Blending

This technique is a great place to start when learning to use brush markers! You apply color directly to paper and use a water brush to blend the colors. The best results come from using a dark, medium, and light hue for each colored section.

Materials

- **Dual brush markers**
- **Water brush, or small round brush and a container of water**
- **Rubber stamp (detailed stamps showing shadows work best)**
- **Smooth watercolor paper**

1. Stamp the image with a black inkpad onto smooth watercolor paper. Add color with the brush tip using feathered strokes. Start with the lightest color, using the shading on the stamped image as a guide.

2. Add the medium color, blending it into the lighter color.

3. Add the darkest color. It's okay to leave some spaces white. With florals, add a bit of the flower color, the lightest hue, into the leaves and stems.

4. Use the water brush to blend the colors for a soft dark-to-light blend. Do not over-blend. You will know if you are over-blending if the paper starts to pill or your colors lose the dark and light contrast. Touch the tip of the brush to a piece of paper towel to remove excess water before blending.

Freehand "DoodleDab" Drawing

You can make freehand drawings with brush markers, too! Check out this technique, called "DoodleDabs." A simple dabbing motion creates a teardrop-shaped stroke, which is the basis of all the designs, alongside several other useful strokes. Master these strokes and you will be able to accent cards, scrapbook pages, envelopes, and more! The DoodleDab technique was designed using Tombow Dual Brush Markers—the nylon brush tip is strong and will stand up to the dabbing action, stroke after stroke.

Basic Teardrop Stroke

Dab the brush tip onto the paper to make the teardrop stroke. It's that simple! Apply lighter pressure for smaller strokes and heavier pressure for larger strokes. It's usually easiest to make teardrop strokes with the point facing away from you.

Two-Toned Teardrop Stroke

To make a two-toned teardrop stroke, choose two colors, one darker than the other. Add a few strokes of the darker color onto a smooth plastic blending palette. Pick up this color with a lighter colored marker by dragging the brush tip through the color. Make the teardrop stroke, and you will have magically created a perfectly blended two-toned mark. (When finished, clean the lighter marker by making a few strokes on a piece of scrap paper until the darker color is gone.)

Lines and Dots

These marks are created with the fine tip of the marker. They are great for delicate standalone details as well as details inside larger areas of color.

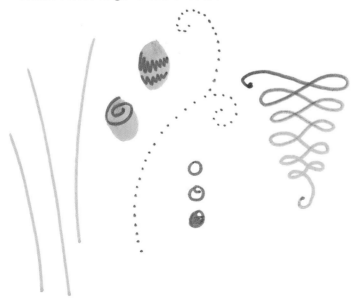

Other Strokes

Here are a few other strokes to create different designs and to accent the basic teardrop strokes. Experiment with applying different amounts of pressure with the marker and using various color combinations.

Cone stroke: Place the brush tip onto the paper horizontally and make the teardrop stroke while flicking the pen downwards to create the cone shape.

Oval stroke: Place the brush tip onto the paper and make a tiny circle while applying pressure on the tip (top row). This creates the oval shape and, when you have two colors on the marker, creates a beautiful two-toned oval.

Long stroke: Drag the brush tip down to make this stroke. Apply different amounts of pressure to vary the thickness of the stroke. If you lift the marker off the paper with a flick, you will create a point on the top.

Varied stroke: Vary the thickness of this stroke by applying light pressure for a thin mark and heavier pressure for a thick mark. You can make this stroke slowly, but do not hesitate in the middle of the stroke.

Marie Browning is a gifted craft designer and artist. She is the author of *Time to Tangle with Colors, Pencil Magic,* and *Brush Marker Magic,* from which this article was adapted. *Brush Marker Magic* sells for $12.99 and is available to order (see page 77) or to purchase in craft and bookstores everywhere.

Powder Room Caddy Set

No more messes in the bathroom! This adorable trio, which includes a jewelry holder and two storage containers, will add a pop of style to your powder room. The creative design utilizes inexpensive clay flower pots to create charming storage caddies. Color your design to match your bathroom décor.

Materials

- Colored design (pattern on page 83)
- 1 clay pot, tall
- 1 clay pot, small
- 2 clay pot saucers, sized to match the diameter of the tall pot mouth
- 1 glass knob
- High gloss blue paint
- Decoupage medium
- Paintbrush
- Hot glue and gun

Project pattern by Jess Volinski

1. **Prepare your coloring sheet.** Find the coloring template and cut the designs to size. Color using your choice of colors and medium (we used standard coloring markers).

2. **Paint.** Paint all the pots and saucers with high gloss blue paint. Work in thin layers to ensure that the paint does not drip. Apply two coats, allowing the paint to dry thoroughly between coats. Allow the pots to dry completely.

3. **Add the designs.** Working with one flower at a time, cover the back with decoupage medium and adhere to each pot. Be sure to make one saucer with the flower on the underside. Once all of your flowers are arranged, go over all the pot surfaces with decoupage medium. Allow the decoupage to dry before adding one more coat of decoupage all over.

4. **Add the knob.** Apply a dot of hot glue in the center of the flower on the saucer with the flower on the underside. Press the bottom of the glass knob onto the glue and allow it to dry. Monitor the knob to ensure it does not slide, adjusting as necessary. When everything is totally dry, fill your containers with cotton swabs, cotton balls, and jewelry.

Keep Calm and Color On!

Nature Mandalas
Coloring Book
$9.99 • Code: DO5492

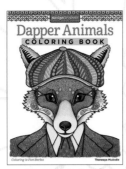

Dapper Animals
Coloring Book
$9.99 • Code: DO5493

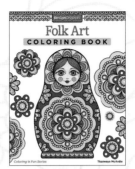

Folk Art
Coloring Book
$9.99 • Code: DO5494

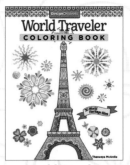

World Traveler
Coloring Book
$9.99 • Code: DO5495

Day of the Dead
Coloring Book
$9.99 • Code: DO5496

Groovy Abstract
Coloring Book
$9.99 • Code: DO5497

Peace & Love
Coloring Book
$9.99 • Code: DO5498

Hipster
Coloring Book
$9.99 • Code: DO5499

Happy Campers
Coloring Book
$9.99 • Code: DO5500

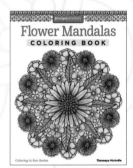

Flower Mandalas
Coloring Book
$9.99 • Code: DO5529

Good Vibes
Coloring Book
$9.99 • Code: DO5530

Follow Your Bliss
Coloring Book
$9.99 • Code: DO5531

Free Spirit
Coloring Book
$9.99 • Code: DO5532

FloraBunda Style
$19.99 • Code: DO5526

FloraBunda Basics
$12.99 • Code: DO5527

FloraBunda Woodland
$12.99 • Code: DO5544

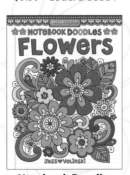

Notebook Doodles
Flowers
$7.99 • Code: DO5549

Notebook Doodles
Go Girl!
$7.99 • Code: DO5550

Notebook Doodles
Fabulous Fashion
$7.99 • Code: DO5551

TangleEasy Wildlife
Designs
$14.99 • Code: DO5562
Visit *TangleEasy.com* for
more great patterns!

BOOKS for Coloring Creativity

Creative Coloring Flowers
$9.99 • Code: DO5505

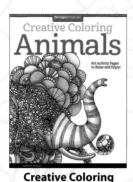

Creative Coloring Animals
$9.99 • Code: DO5506

Creative Coloring Inspirations
$9.99 • Code: DO5507

Creative Coloring Mandalas
$9.99 • Code: DO5508

Creative Coloring Birds
$9.99 • Code: DO5538

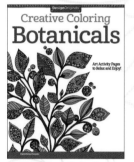

Creative Coloring Botanicals
$9.99 • Code: DO5539

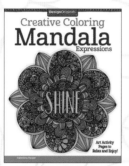

Creative Coloring Mandala Expressions
$9.99 • Code: DO5540

Creative Coloring Patterns of Nature
$9.99 • Code: DO5541

Fun & Funky Coloring Book Treasury
$19.99 • Code: DO5556

Don't Worry, Be Happy Coloring Book Treasury
$19.99 • Code: DO5557

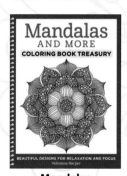

Mandalas and More Coloring Book Treasury
$19.99 • Code: DO5558

Ultimate Coloring Book Treasury
$19.99 • Code: DO5559

Color Joy Coloring Book
$4.99 • Code: DO5566

Color Zen Coloring Book
$4.99 • Code: DO5567

Color Calm Coloring Book
$4.99 • Code: DO5568

Color Fun Coloring Book
$4.99 • Code: DO5569

Color Love Coloring Book
$4.99 • Code: DO5570

Color Dream Coloring Book
$4.99 • Code: DO5571

Pixel Gamer Coloring Book
$4.99 • Code: DO5577

Pixel Power Coloring Book
$4.99 • Code: DO5576

DESIGN ORIGINALS

By Phone: 800-457-9112 • **Direct:** 717-560-4703
Fax: 717-560-4702
Online at: www.FoxChapelPublishing.com
By Mail: Send Check or Money Order to
Fox Chapel Publishing
1970 Broad St.
East Petersburg, PA 17520

US

# Item	Shipping Rate
1 Item	$3.99
Each Additional	.99

Canadian & International Orders - please email
info@foxchapelpublishing.com or
visit our website for actual shipping costs.

VISA • Master Card • DISCOVER NOVUS

Zentangle® Can Change Your Life!

Zentangle Basics, Expanded Workbook Edition
$8.99 • Code: DO5462

Zentangle 2, Expanded Workbook Edition
$8.99 • Code: DO5468

Zentangle 3, Expanded Workbook Edition
$8.99 • Code: DO5469

Zentangle 4, Expanded Workbook Edition
$8.99 • Code: DO5489

Zentangle 5, Expanded Workbook Edition
$8.99 • Code: DO5490

Zentangle 6, Expanded Workbook Edition
$8.99 • Code: DO5488

Zentangle 7, Expanded Workbook Edition
$8.99 • Code: DO5485

Zentangle 8, Expanded Workbook Edition
$8.99 • Code: DO5463

Zentangle 9, Workbook Edition
$8.99 • Code: DO3517

Zentangle 10, Workbook Edition
$8.99 • Code: DO3510

Zentangle 11, Workbook Edition
$8.99 • Code: DO5521

Zentangle 12, Workbook Edition
$8.99 • Code: DO5555

Zen Quilting Workbook, Revised Edition
$18.99 • Code: DO5548

Zen-sational Stitches for Quilting
$18.99 • Code: DO5377

Zentangle Fabric Arts
$16.99 • Code: DO5366

BOOKS for Zen-Inspired Drawing

Joy of Zentangle
$24.99 • Code: DO5398

The Beauty of Zentangle
$24.99 • Code: DO5038

Time to Tangle with Colors
$16.99 • Code: DO5362

Zen Mandalas
$16.99 • Code: DO5367

Yoga for Your Brain
$16.99 • Code: DO5369

Totally Tangled
$16.99 • Code: DO5360

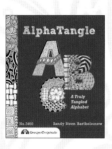

AlphaTangle
$9.99 • Code: DO3460

Tangled Fashionista
$9.99 • Code: DO3492

Zentangle for Kidz!
$8.99 • Code: DO3463

Zenspirations
$16.99 • Code: DO5370

Zenspirations Dangle Designs, Expanded Workbook Edition
$8.99 • Code: DO5461

Zenspirations Coloring Book Flowers
$9.99 • Code: DO5443

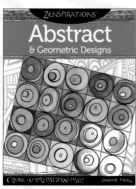

Zenspirations Coloring Book Abstract & Geometric Designs
$9.99 • Code: DO5445

Zenspirations Coloring Book Inspirations
$9.99 • Code: DO5446

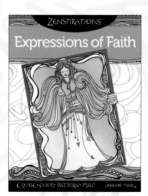

Zenspirations Coloring Book Expressions of Faith
$9.99 • Code: DO5459

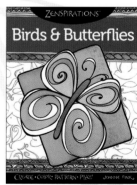

Zenspirations Coloring Book Birds & Butterflies
$9.99 • Code: DO5444

DESIGN ORIGINALS

By Phone: 800-457-9112 • **Direct:** 717-560-4703
Fax: 717-560-4702
Online at: www.FoxChapelPublishing.com
By Mail: Send Check or Money Order to
Fox Chapel Publishing
1970 Broad St.
East Petersburg, PA 17520

US

# Item	Shipping Rate
1 Item	$3.99
Each Additional	.99

VISA
MasterCard
DISCOVER NOVUS

Canadian & International Orders - please email
info@foxchapelpublishing.com or
visit our website for actual shipping costs.

CONTRIBUTORS

Suzanne McNeill

Suzanne McNeill is the author of more than 30 best-selling books, including *Joy of Zentangle*, *The Beauty of Zentangle*, *Zentangle Basics* through *Zentangle 12*, and *Zen Mandalas*. She is a designer, author, columnist, art instructor, and lover of everything hands-on. Her Zentangle-inspired paintings have been called "mesmerizing art." Suzanne founded Design Originals (an imprint of Fox Chapel Publishing), the leading publisher of Zentangle books. She was voted "Designer of the Year" and received the "Lifetime Achievement Award" from the Craft & Hobby Association. blog.suzannemcneill.com / www.SparksStudioArt.com

Kati Erney

Kati Erney works on staff at Design Originals in the book editorial department, where she spends a surprising number of hours crafting. She loves to color in vibrant hues and striking, symmetrical patterns. The first Design Originals book she helped with was *Ice Princess Crafts* in 2014, and she most recently made numerous projects for *Crafting with Clay Pots*. Some of her favorite things include reading books and creating art for home decoration, which makes working at Design Originals a dream.

Joanne Fink

Joanne Fink loves letters, words, and writing inspiring sentiments. An award-winning designer, calligrapher, and author, Joanne has more than 20 years of experience as an art director in the greeting card industry. She specializes in developing products for the gift, stationery, craft, and faith-based markets from her Lakeside Design studio in central Florida. Her Zenspirations® brand has been licensed for many products, including her seven bestselling Zenspirations books from Design Originals in which she teaches her method of patterned drawing. www.zenspirations.com

Thaneeya McArdle

Thaneeya McArdle is the creative force behind the Art is Fun coloring book series from Design Originals. Her bestselling coloring books *Nature Mandalas*, *Happy Campers*, *Day of the Dead*, and others are inspired by her love of travel. She creates her colorful art in a variety of styles. In addition to her 15 published books, her art appears in private collections around the world. She launched her popular website, www.art-is-fun.com, in 2009. Visit her there to get fun lessons on drawing, painting, mixed media, and of course coloring! www.thaneeya.com

Marie Browning

Marie Browning has inspired crafters internationally with her vast knowledge of products and techniques. She is the best-selling author of more than 30 crafting books and has more than 2 million books in print. Her books are available worldwide and printed in numerous languages. Marie's book *Time to Tangle with Colors* features techniques for coloring Zentangle art using Tombow's Dual Brush Pens. Marie writes articles for national craft magazines, teaches hands-on classes, provides live demonstrations, and appears on TV and in videos. www.mariebrowning.com

Ben Kwok

Ben Kwok is a talented, detail-oriented artist and designer who has worked with major brands including Disney, Converse, and Lucky Brand. Inspired by Art Nouveau and Biomechanics, among other art styles, Ben's work is seamless and skillfully executed. He is the creator of Ornation Creation, a Zentangle design group on Facebook, and currently has more than 8,200 followers from around the world. His book *TangleEasy Wildlife Designs* is the first published template book in a series of four, with three more titles coming soon. www.bioworkz.com

Valentina Harper

Valentina Harper is the author/illustrator behind the best-selling Creative Coloring series. One of her titles, *Creative Coloring Inspirations*, has climbed to the top of the Amazon.com and other publishing charts. The Venezuelan artist spends countless hours creating her signature uplifting messages and intricate designs from her studio in Nashville, TN. In addition to the art and products featuring her designs, Valentina's work is showcased on the Spirit Desert collection with Sakroots. www.valentinadesign.com.

Jess Volinski

Jess Volinski is an author, illustrator, hand-letterer, and surface designer. Her new tween coloring book series, Notebook Doodles, is launching this fall in book and craft stores around the country. She received an MFA from School of Visual Arts in New York. Her artwork has appeared on countless products and advertisements, including with the CBS network. www.jessvolinski.com

GOOD TIMES

CHEERS!

with love

ENJOY

CELEBRATE!

JUST FOR YOU

thank you

happy birthday

© DO Magazine and Thaneeya McArdle

© DO Magazine and Jess Volinski

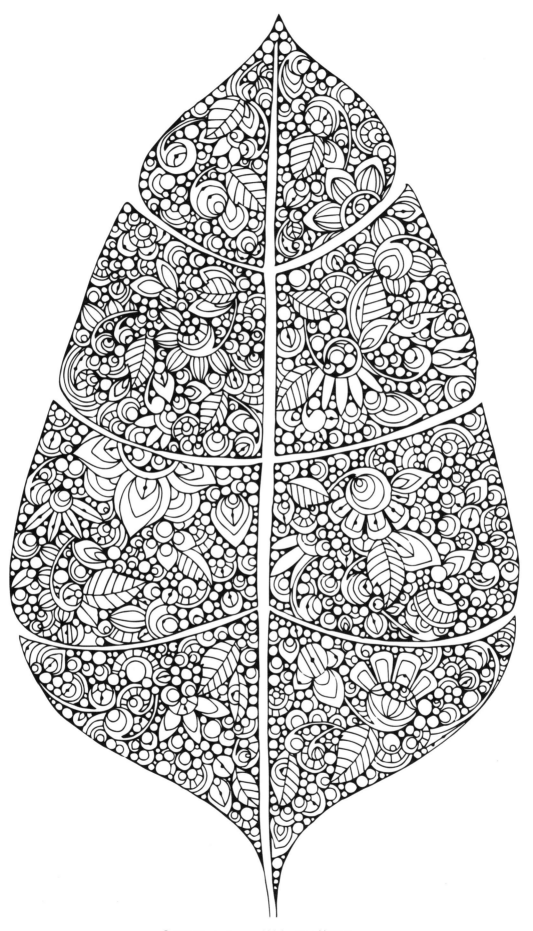

© DO Magazine and Valentina Harper

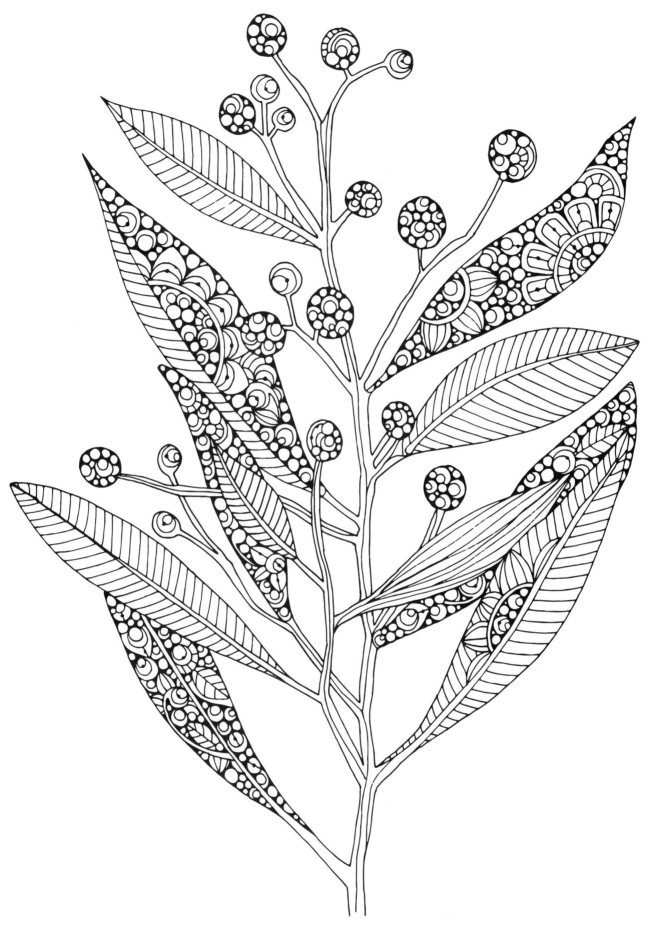

© DO Magazine and Valentina Harper

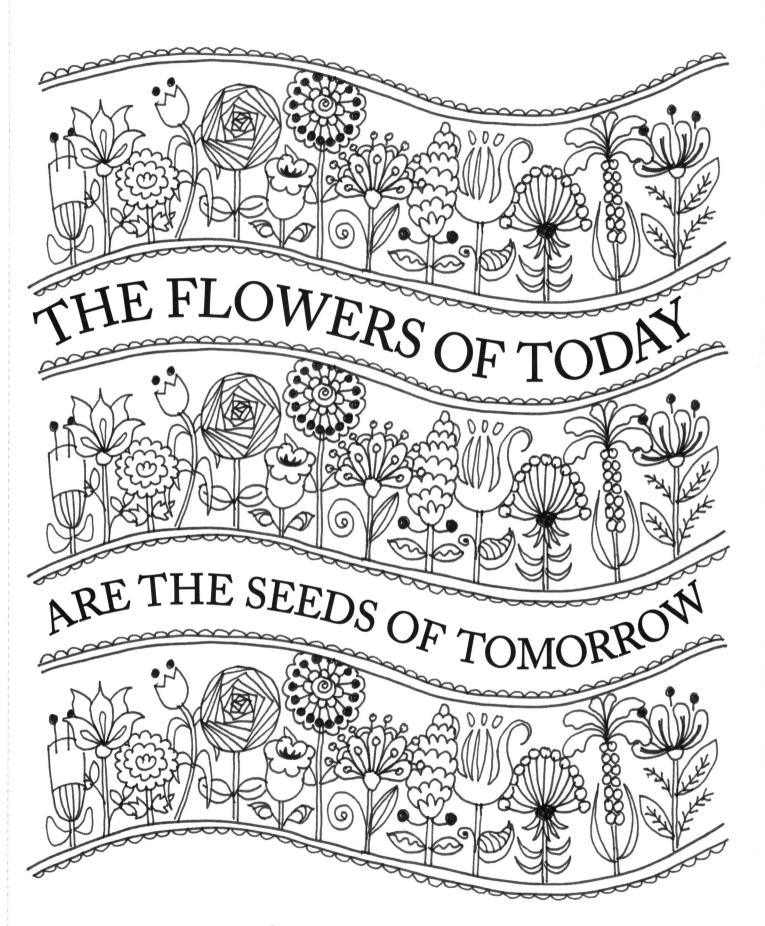

THE FLOWERS OF TODAY

ARE THE SEEDS OF TOMORROW

© DO Magazine and Thaneeya McArdle

LET LOVE GROW

© DO Magazine and Valentina Harper